BUBBLE GUM SCIENCE

KLUTZ.

Book manufactured in Taiwan; gum, Canada. Double Bubble is a registered trademark of Fleer Confection.

Development: Tien Huyn-Dinh, Robert Young

Pointless Involvement: John Cassidy

Design: Kevin Plottner

Photo Research: Marilyn Green

Acknowledgments:

Paul Doherty, Michael Glass, and the following champion bubble gummers at Berendo Middle School in Los Angeles: Eric Domingo, Fernando Salan, Laura Teague, Ozwaldo Nava.

Thanks to Michael Sherman for cover assistance.

All photos by Peter Fox except the following: page 1, planet Jupiter, NASA; page 17, clockwise from right, Underwood Photo Archives, Art Resource, Peter Fox, Academy Foundation; page 19, NASA; page 20, © Renee Lynn, Tony Stone Images; pages 24 and 25, The Bettmann Archive; page 26, FPG International; page 29, Gary Mcdonald.

Write us:

Klutz is an independent publisher located in Palo Alto, California, and staffed entirely by real human beings. We would love to hear your comments regarding this or any of our books.

455 Portage Avenue
Palo Alto, California 94306

Additional Copies:

For the location of your nearest Klutz retailer, call (650) 857-0888. Should they be tragically out of stock, additional copies of this book, as well as the entire library of "100% Klutz certified" books, are available in our mail order catalogue. See back page.

4 1 5 8 5 7 0 8 8 8

ISBN 1-57054-134-5

BUBBLE GUM BASICS

How to Blow a Bubble

For best results, use fresh bubble gum. The kind that you got last Halloween isn't as good. The sugar actually hurts the process, so, if you want champion bubbles, chew your gum for at least 5 minutes before starting. The key is to get an even, well-chewed, unsugary "film" of gum right in the front of your mouth. Poke a little starting spot with your tongue and blow with a sure and steady stream of air. Good luck.

How to Blow a **Double** Bubble **Double**

Blowing a large bubble — and then blowing a smaller bubble inside of the big one — is something that only 2 percent of modern North American 4th graders can do. In other countries, where kids get more homework and study harder, the percentage is much higher. Here are the steps:

1 Start chewing on three normal chunks of bubble gum.

2 Chew the sugar away and soften the gum (can take as long as 20 minutes).

3 Blow a great bubble — not huge — maybe 6–8 inches, but one that you know you could blow a lot bigger if you wanted. But don't. Seal it off, and immediately begin blowing the second one. THIS IS NOT EASY! Our local champion worked at it for 30 minutes before he got one for us.

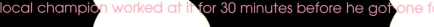

How to Blow a **Triple** Bubble
Triple
Triple

Throughout history, there have been rumors and reports of triple bubbles (the blowing of a bubble within a bubble within a bubble). Scientists used to think that these rumors were no more than myths, and that triple bubbles were simply beyond the reach of human abilities. But in recent years, at least one bubble gum champ has been able to perform "the triple" with breathtaking reliability. We are awed by this knowledge. If you are able to send us a photograph of a bona fide "triple" bubble, in the wild, include your address in the accompanying letter. We will fly there immediately.

What's the trick?

You have to be a fanatic, but if you can do a double reliably, you're at least at the starting gate.

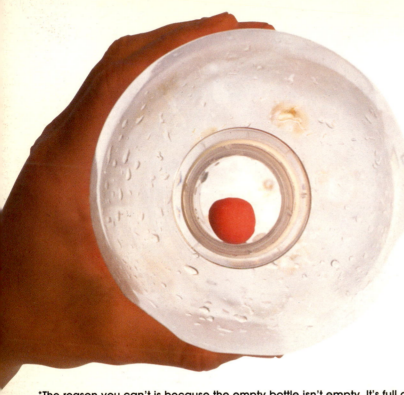

Bubble Gum Blast

Take a pea-shaped wad of gum and place it in the neck of a soda bottle. Then, blow very hard into the bottle. See if you can get the gum to go into the bottle.*

Don't put your mouth <u>on</u> the bottle, but blow hard from an inch or so away.

*The reason you can't is because the empty bottle isn't empty. It's full of air. So the lungful of air that you're trying to blow into the bottle won't fit.

Bubble Gum Up-and-Down

If you drop a pea-sized piece of chewed bubble gum into a glass of water (half-full), it will sink to the bottom. Big surprise. However, if you then add a little bit of clear soda pop, bubbles will appear clinging to the gum and in a few seconds the gum will rise to the surface, carried up by all the bubbles. At the top, the bubbles will pop and the gum will sink. But before it hits the bottom, another crop of bubbles will form all over it and send it back up again. Once it's back to the surface, all the bubbles will burst again, and down it goes again. But before it hits the bottom, another crop of bubbles will form and...
THIS GOES ON FOR HOURS!

Bubble gum submarine, endlessly going up and down

What's the Difference Between Gum **Before** and **After** Chewing?

First of all, it looks worse. You know that. But, from a scientific point of view, what happens? In other words, does it get heavier (because of all your saliva in it) or lighter because of the taste that leaves it? We hired three professional kids to weigh three wads of gum, chew them, then weigh them all again. Here is what we found:

Between 60 percent and 75 percent of a piece of bubble gum (by weight) is sugar. The sugarless kind will lose about 50 percent of its mass in 10 minutes of chewing.

Swallowing Gum

What happens if you eat your chewing gum? First of all, we don't like to talk about this sort of thing, so don't do it and the situation will never come up. However, if you do, it should be unchanged, out of your body and on its way within a few days.

Cracking Gum

VERY important gum skill to learn. Unfortunately, it's basically impossible to teach in a book. The idea is to trap little air bubbles into the gum and then pop them by smushing them against your gums. If you don't know this skill, ask the kid next to you in homeroom. Experienced gum crackers can be a little irritating. Very skilled gum crackers are flat-out scary. Susan Williams, perhaps the leading gum cracker of all time, was once mistaken for gunfire and arrested in a courthouse in Fresno, California.

A Prize-Winning Bubble Gum Science Project

What you'll need:

- A few different kinds of bubble gum
- A few pieces of poster board
- Three unbiased, gum-chewing volunteers

Make three (or more) wild guesses like the following:

Yes   No

① Do Bubble Gum bubbles ever exceed 8 inches in diameter? ☐ ☐

② Does Flabberblabber gum make the biggest bubbles? ☐ ☐

③. Is Slimy brand bubble gum the best tasting? ☐ ☐

④. Does Bubble gum flavor all go away within 3 minutes? ☐ ☐

Since these are only guesses, you're going to have to prove (or disprove) them scientifically. How? Experiments. Plus graphs (science teachers love graphs). For question number ① , give each volunteer three pieces of bubble gum (same brand) and tell them to go for their biggest bubble. To measure big bubbles, we use a homemade pair of "scissors" made out of two rulers. If you make something like this, call them "calipers" (it's more accurate and will look better on your report anyway). After your volunteers have done their big bubble best with one brand of gum, switch to another. And another. Record your results every time.

Measure the diameter with "calipers." (They're like big scissors.)

Bubble Sizes

bubble diameter 1" 2" 3" 4"

Flabber ⟶

Slimy ⟶

Yechhy ⟶

For question number ②, which brand is the best tasting, get your volunteers to close their eyes. Unwrap the gum and stick a piece of the same brand in each of their mouths. Get them to rate the flavor on a scale of 1-10. Then, do the same with two or three other leading brands. Record your results.

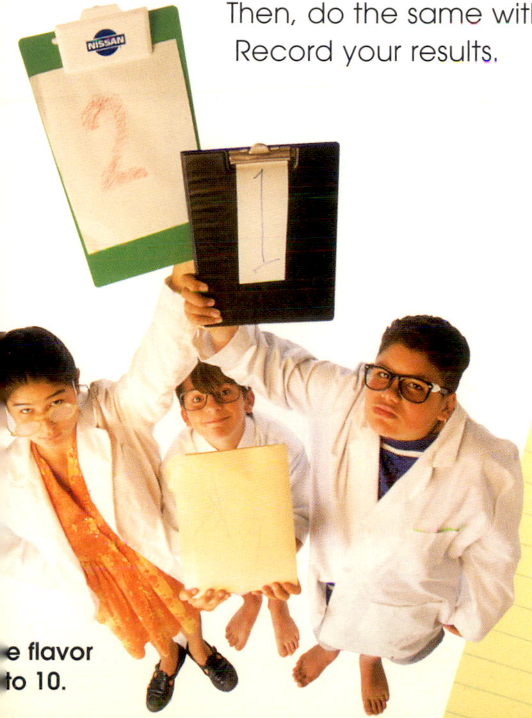

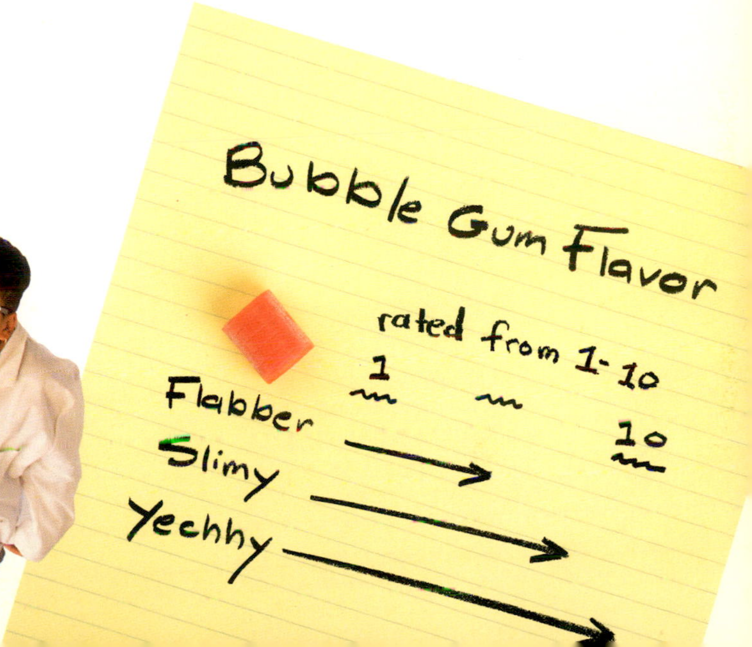

e flavor
to 10.

Bubble Gum Flavor

rated from 1-10
1 ~   ~   10 ~

Flabber
Slimy
Yechhy

For question number **3**, how long does the flavor last, use a watch. Volunteers need to raise their hand as soon as their bubble gum has lost all of its flavor. For extra credit: Do this several times, always with different brands.

Raise your hand as soon as the flavor is gone.

BIG HINT **On Displaying Your Results:**

On your poster board, put your guesses at the top. Describe your experiments, and record your results using graphs liberally. And be sure to take a photograph of your biggest bubble as it is being measured.

BUBBLE GUM FACTOIDS

● Which is more popular in the U.S. and Canada? Chewing gum? Or bubble gum? Answer: Chewing gum (although bubble gum is gaining). In the mid-50s, chewing gum was 10 times more popular. Today, it's only 3 times.

● Mexico, where bubble gum is more popular than chewing gum, is the home of Pow Wow brand bubble gum, which has a hot chili pepper center.

● What's the best way to get gum off clothes? Rub the spot with ice. When the gum hardens, scrape it off.

● Where is it illegal to chew gum? Singapore, where nasty fines exist if you're caught chewing in public.

A Brief Bubble Gum History

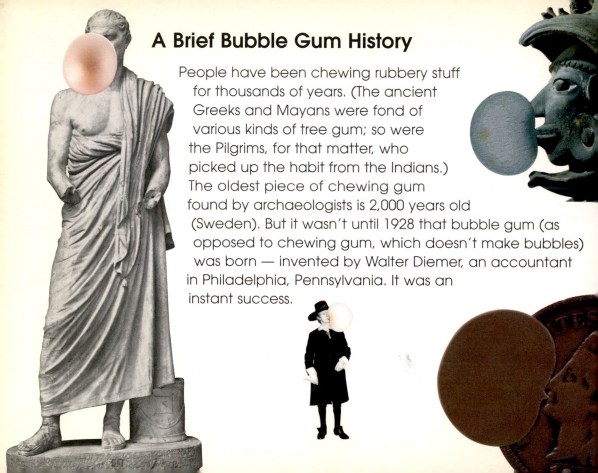

People have been chewing rubbery stuff for thousands of years. (The ancient Greeks and Mayans were fond of various kinds of tree gum; so were the Pilgrims, for that matter, who picked up the habit from the Indians.) The oldest piece of chewing gum found by archaeologists is 2,000 years old (Sweden). But it wasn't until 1928 that bubble gum (as opposed to chewing gum, which doesn't make bubbles) was born — invented by Walter Diemer, an accountant in Philadelphia, Pennsylvania. It was an instant success.

● **How do you get bubble gum off your face after your bubble has popped?** Take the rest of the gum from your mouth and dab the smeary mess off with that.

● **How much do North American kids spend on bubble gum every year?** About half a billion dollars. (That's half a "billion," not million.) That translates to 40 million pieces of bubble gum chewed every day, 1.6 million pieces every hour, 26,000 pieces every minute and 444 every second.

● **From about 1950 to 1990 baseball cards were included with bubble gum.** At first, the cards were just thrown into the package in an effort to make the gum more interesting. Almost immediately kids began collecting the cards. By 1980, the cards had become so popular that kids were throwing away the gum and keeping the cards as the whole collector market boomed. In 1991, the biggest card manufacturer dropped the gum out of the package entirely, because collectors were complaining that the gum damaged the cards.

For the same reason a cat curls up in a ball or a planet is round. Being round is the laziest way nature has to enclose a given amount of space. It's the most economical and requires the least amount of energy.

The **Biggest** Bubble Ever?

According to the Guinness Book of World Records, the biggest bubble ever blown was 22 inches in diameter (Susan Williams, Fresno, California, 1985).

22"

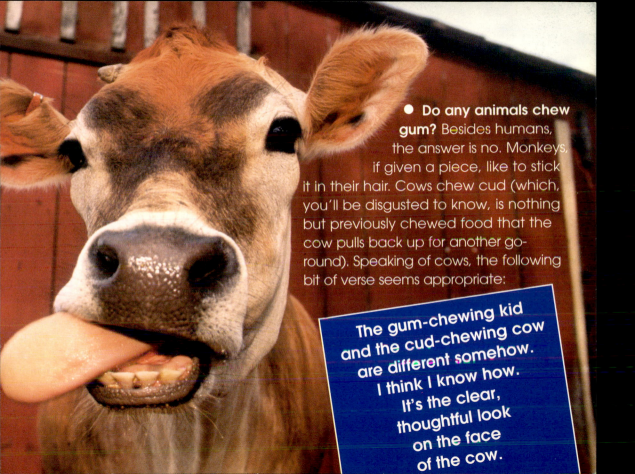

● **Do any animals chew gum?** Besides humans, the answer is no. Monkeys, if given a piece, like to stick it in their hair. Cows chew cud (which, you'll be disgusted to know, is nothing but previously chewed food that the cow pulls back up for another go-round). Speaking of cows, the following bit of verse seems appropriate:

The gum-chewing kid
and the cud-chewing cow
are different somehow.
I think I know how.
It's the clear,
thoughtful look
on the face
of the cow.

The Bubble Gum String
Stretch
Challenge

Here at Klutz Galactic Headquarters we were able to take one piece of bubble gum as shown, chew it thoroughly, and then stretch it into a string 6 feet long. If you are able to match or exceed this record, we would appreciate your dropping us a card since we don't think it can be done and we will probably need to see a photo (unretouched) as well as an affidavit signed by your parent, legal guardian or notary public.

KLUTZ
Bubblegum Challenge
455 Portage Ave.
Palo Alto, CA 94306

Be a Bubble Gum
Detective

You're a detective checking out a crime scene. You find a bubble gum wrapper and, nearby, a shoeprint belonging to the criminal. From the print you can see that he stepped on a wad of gum. What can you say about the criminal?

Answer: He's a 135-pound near-sighted slob with a tattoo on his left bicep that reads "Go Cal."

How did you know all that?

Elementary.

1 You figured out his weight from the size of the bubble gum splat that was stuck to the bottom of his shoe. You knew how much and what kind of gum the guy was chewing from the wrapper you found, and the bigger the splat, the heavier the guy, so all you had to do was get a few different-sized volunteers to step on gum until one of them matched.

2 You knew he was near-sighted because he stepped on a wad of gum.

3 You knew he was a slob because he threw it on the ground in the first place.

4 And the tattoo? That was just a guess.

The Stepped-On Bubble Gum Scale

200 pounds

50 pounds

100 pounds

140 pounds

The Story of Chewing Gum `or` Whatever Happened to the Guy Who Killed Davy Crockett?

In Texas anyway, it's a pretty well-known fact that the leader of the Mexican army that overran the Alamo, Jim Bowie, Davy Crockett and the rest of its glorious defenders, was the infamous General Santa Anna. But what's not so well known is that afterwards, General Santa Anna had a mid-life career change (not entirely his own choice). He got out of the military and into the tree sap business.

Davy Crockett

A few years after his Alamo experiences, former General Santa Anna was in New York. He had with him a large quantity of sapodilla tree sap (otherwise known as chicle). The sapodilla is a tree common in the jungles of

General Santa Anna

Mexico, Central and South America where the natives had been chewing on wads of its sap for thousands of years. (In North America, the natives were no less fond of chewing things, they just used spruce or pine resin instead.)

But Santa Anna had far more practical things in mind than munching on tree sap. He was hoping that some ingenious Yankee would be able to refine the chicle into a cheap substitute for rubber.

One man he approached was Thomas Adams, a New Jersey inventor who experimented with chicle for some time before giving up in frustration and tossing the stuff into his scrap pile. It was a dark hour for the future of chewing gum. Fortunately, Adams had a young son and (according to legend) it was he who rescued it from the scrap heap and popped it into his mouth.

When his father discovered his son gnawing away on the stuff, a lightbulb went on. Chewing gum was far from unknown at the time (desperate North Americans were using tree resin, wax or whale blubber), but Adams knew a better mousetrap when he saw one.

Th
A
th
b
c
g

Adams

New York
napping & Stretching

Gum

a year, "Adams New
apping and Stretching
was on the market
oring a big success
ially after it became
d with sarsaparilla).

What About Today's Chewing Gum?

In these chemical days, of course, chewing gum has nothing to do with Mexican trees, but is actually flavored, sweetened food-grade plastics. Better chewing through modern science.

If you're ever in San Luis Obispo, California... For more than 40 years, thousands of people have come to a single little alley in a small coastal town in California to stick their bubble gum to the walls of its buildings. It's known unofficially and legendarily as Bubble Gum Alley.

Who Are You? (You wonderful person you)

❏ Kid ❏ Grown-up ❏ In-between ❏ Girl ❏ Boy

Name _____

Address _____

City _____ State _____ Zip _____

How did you first hear about BUBBLE GUM SCIENCE? _____

_____

True or False

❏ T ❏ F Someone gave me this book as a gift because they like me a whole lot!

❏ T ❏ F I bought this book for myself because I deserve it!

❏ T ❏ F This is the first **KLUTZ** book I've ever gotten.

A Personal Question! I'm the kind of person who spends this kind of money on a gift for a friend: ❏ Less than $10 ❏ $10–$15 ❏ $15–$20 ❏ $20–25 ❏ For the right gift, whatever it's worth!

My Bright Ideas What would you like us to write a book about?

_____

Write your complaints here. ❏ (Please don't go outside the box.)

Cut out
Fill in
Add stamp
Mail
Wait
Impatiently

BUBBLE GUM SCIENCE

First Class
Postage
Here

Catalogue
455 Portage Avenue
Palo Alto, CA 94306